A collection of poems from transitional and salutary journeys

Poems for life's journeys

LINDA HUXLEY

Heddon Publishing

First edition published in 2025 by Heddon Publishing.

Copyright © Linda Huxley 2025, all rights reserved.
No part of this book may be reproduced, adapted, stored in a retrieval system or transmitted by any means, electronic, photocopying, or otherwise without prior permission of the author.

ISBN 978-1-917824-05-7
(ebook 978-1-917824-06-4)

Cover design by Catherine Clarke Design

This is a work of creativity and fiction. Names, characters, businesses, places, events and incidents are either the products of the author's imagination or used in a fictitious manner. Any resemblance to actual persons, living or dead, or actual events is purely coincidental.

www.heddonpublishing.com
www.facebook.com/heddonpublishing
@PublishHeddon

Salomé
Salomé

Dedicated to Rob, my co-pilot in my life's journeys.

Contents

Journeys back home
   Bread of Home 11
   Food Love Story 13
   Reasons to Cry for Spilt Milk 14
   Domesticity, Reasons to Travel 15
   Kitchen-phobias 16
   Hygge 18
   Back in Time 19

Away
   Winter Solstice Long Past 23
   Christmases 24
   Joe ponders 25

Journey to Selfhood
   The Body's wisdom 31
   Matriarchy 32
   Lost and Found 36
   Found and Lost 37

Away to School
   Boarding at Mystic House School 41
   It already has 44

Heroes and Camp Followers
   Hero Worship 47
   All the amazing ones that I will not be 48

From a Family Album 49
   Female Suffrage 51
   Great Grandmother Louise, Poverty 52

    Beating rugs and Hitler 53
    My Aunty, The Peace Warrior 56
    They have your heart 58
Religiosity and Faith
    Fool's choices 63
    Salt, Psalter and sacrilege 64
    Riddle 67
    The Impossibility of Faith 70
    Mental Health and Fundamentalism in the 1970s 71
    The sheer weight of things 73
Fanciful Time Travel
    Hey Diddle Diddle 77
    Baby, I may be biased? 78
    The Eighth 79
    Noah before the rainbow 81
    Three Troublesome Old Men 83
    Old Mother Time 85
    One Tree Hill 87
    Un-pathetic fallacy poem 2020 89
Off To War
    Warr Meets Peace 93
    Tyne Cot 95
    Forgive 96
    The March 97
Walks and Wanderings
    Winter Spell 103
    Autumn's dance 104
    A disturbance 106
    Too much Awesomeness in Banff 108

Journeys to Creativity
   The Cynic's Guide to Art? 111
   Poems – catch 'em before they fly 112
   The Poet 113
   The Muse 114

Journeys Home
   When I should go 117
   Blessings 119

Notes from the author 121
Thank yous 125

Journeys back home

Bread of Home

Slow soured Poolish, Rye or Pumpernickel
loaves, signed with the cross or slit like a kipper,
mouthy crunch yields to softness and flavour
from air, water, fire and stone,
to sustain or solely to savour.
Focaccia, Tortilla, Pita, Soda,
Challah, Khobez, Muffin, Rota.

Soft showers of sifted grain
falling and turning into air
a bridal veil like angel's hair
(till wetted and wedded to lecherous
and hoochy old yeast's pungent froth and belch.)
Kneading till silky, needs folding and rolling,
sticky hand-shaping, patient pulling and coaxing,
feeding and guarding, celebrating every golden
burling bubble, as each miracle inflates and doubles,
and begets dough!

This rustic symphony, this alchemy of plasticity
becomes a masseured marvel of domesticity.
Each slap and spread lifts flaccidness
to life, each stretch, each plaiting, primping
and pinching becoming rife and
forms that amber window to view
the waiting oven or hot-coals through.

Sweetly sour meets salt, a tiny peck, added last,
speaking of sea and sands, savour and bite,
then dough rewards the heat with bread so crisp,
and light, for every hearty, home-coming repast.

Food Love Story

(After listening to too many food programmes)

Food is a consummate joy.
Don't'ya envy my new cooking toy?
From Colcannon, 'Begorra',
To Paneer or Pakora,
Our pleasure just doesn't alloy.

Food is an absolute pain.
Stuffing ourselves and yet eating again?
To allay my sweet tooth
Carb scores shoot through the roof
With cholesterol that puts me to shame.

A remedy and a sure cause
For all't ails us, of course.
We must love our biomes
While consuming rhizomes,
And never eat pig, cow or horse.

*(Only fungi or vegetable 'meat'
created and cultured in a lab?)*

Reasons to Cry for Spilt Milk

One, the breast milk is yours
and you're leaving a howling baby.

Two, milk spilt is from the very last cow
(and there will be a last cow)
and that cow has gone missing…

Three, your world's collapsed
with the spilt milk (and all you needed was a
cup-of-strong-milky-tea).

Four, the knowledge that time cannot
work backwards and milk,
once so dispersed, can never
be put back in that bottle.

Five, when it is the last drop
you'll ever know of the milk
of human kindness, of course.

Domesticity, Reasons to Travel

I spent two hours descaling the bathroom,
one hour on the friggin' stairs.
I bought a brush
with a spinning head
now twizzle on that if you dare.

I splashed out on t'power steamer,
a tall brush and some 'Zim',
a tool that excavates the grout,
and two for 'neath the rim.

See if this product shifts the grease
or whitens window stains
if limescale dissolveth in a flash
or pesky mould remains.

So, at my funeral they can say,
(whatever they say beside)
how "she always scoured 'er chiffonier
and 'ad a sparkling underside."

Kitchen-phobias

A poem for anyone who had a 1950s suburban childhood where every kitchen appliance seemed to be out to get you and injuries abounded.
Each housewife skilfully learnt to avoid burns and scalds and flattened fingers from the washing mangle. A kitchen was the place where all of life happened and chip pans daily caught fire and pressure cookers vented boiling hot steam or food geysers. Because of the prevalence of contagious diseases, hankies, pants, sanitary-ware and nappies were boiled or burned. Brawn from pig's heads, roast hearts, liver, tripe and kidneys made delicious meals from rather horrific looking contents.

Boiling vats of melted snot,
tripe'n onions cooked in the pot,
bald suet puddings wrapped up in strings,
head up my list of vile kitchen-esque things.
Mincers and mangles and meaty farragoes
of liver and lights with cooking fandangos.
Oh space-ship hair dryer! Home perming solution!
A sizzling hair fryer! All beauty tuition?
The stove that burnt the 'bunnies',
the curling tongs that singed,
the pressure cooker hissed and spat,
the iron that scorched my things.
A 'cruelty' of kitchen knives,
a chip pan catching fire,

a mouse in a trap with seven lives,
green light from the Frigidaire
reveals innocent porky trotters
and the pig's head's vacant glare.

Hygge

(Hygge: a Danish word conveying the sense of cosy home comforts and relaxation with those you love.)

My friend told me how she was preparing
the house for winter.
I visualised houses in scarves and cosy jumpers.
My mind saw streets with fleeces
and roof-shaped hats.
Wax candles flickered, lit
to light the good worker home,
attracting light-winged moths,
daintily dressed house mice,
and look, a family holding hands around the table
for evening prayers before the steaming soup.

Back in Time

I dreamed I held it still,
Brass Lion,
cool and heavy in my hand,
tasting the colour, hearing the shine.

In a toy farmyard, another lion,
his appearance a wonder!
Orange Lion,
toting tiny, wonky, plastic glasses.

Those lions! Oh, the prowling
prowess of their lines
Oh! The tremble of their growl.

Presence and protection,
unquestioned play-champions
of my childhood stories.
From Grandma's bronze mantelpiece,
the ash-tray slipper, the brooding spider,
the nutcracker crocodile,
Brass Lion with the Blenheim sword,
were martial ornaments frozen on parade.

Orange Lion was our toy-box team player.
How did he disappear?
Up the metal gullet while vacuuming?

Down the throat of our golden Labrador?
In my dream I found and held them fast
and was once more a child.

Away

Winter Solstice Long Past

From heart of forest to Great Hall,
we haul a tree to ward off night.
For the fire, a log to banish dark
and fill the home with warmth and light.

From the shortest day to the longest eve
we look towards each unwound year.
The sun will dance and we will steer
our lives before Time's (lifted) scythe.

Christmases

Christmas is best for Happy Families
Mr Bunn the Baker, Mrs Green the Grocer.
Games for wheelers and traders
dealers and raiders, charaders and actors
picture-ites and party obfuscators.

Christmas is good for passion, for werewolf love
     bites,
fly-by nights and under-the-mistletoe rights
     unrationed.
For mice in cheese and jolly children up all night,
Calling, 'Santa, fill my stocking pleeease!'

Christmas is not the kindest
to the lonely or forsaken
or with eating dis-harmonies
whose meagre income is taken.
Worst, for the old, unwell, those whose feet swell
and whose neglected hearts dwell
in the past where Christmas magic reigns still.

Joe ponders

We chose a good donkey;
clean, no signs of mange.
Sound hooves and back,
only a bit crowd-shy,
and not a brayer.

You wouldn't have recognised
Bethlehem
As country folk we were happiest anyway
In the adobe shed,
not too draughty,
with only one bit of thatch missing
and open to the stars.

Its hairy inhabitants
I swear,
were better behaved
than those carousing
In the Inn.

The good-natured Ox made room,
chomping, rumbling, farting
and rhythmically pacing
in his stall –
as if he wanted part of it.

The tan milch cow (calf suckling),
goats untethered,
were well mannered as could be,
udders bulging with free milk,
pied kids climbing bales to see
with their horizontal eyes a slant.

A Nubian woman came
when it was time
to aid my wife.
Birth a bit premature
(after all that bumping,)
and our baby impatient to emerge
gave little trouble for a first-born.

Too beautiful he seemed
to follow my rough trade.
We shared our tale
with sweet Nazarene Wine.
She was the first to behold him
and lift her hands in praise.

Strangely he had
my late father's look,
his stately head and nose.
A relief to claim him of the line of David
(though gossips will have their say.)

Shoe-less, the sheep-herding youth
appeared soon after
mumbling about angel song?
Mary liked him straight-way.
He had that same look
in his eyes that Mary had
since that visitation.

And who was I, a simple man to fathom or to
        question?
We stayed a while visiting family,
a rare treat in these tough tax-us-to-the-bone times.

Never had a commoner's infant son
        caused such commotion.
The wooden cradle left in my workshop
(decorated with jumping deer and fowl)
could never have been as admired as
when dear Mary made our child at home,
upon the beast's fresh hay
for all who came to see.

As we were packing,
on the twelfth eve,
three visitors, royalty all,
had been summoned to the stall.
They knew somehow, rich gifts to bring.

Frankincense oil – for a god-king,
midwife to passing souls.
Oil of Myrrh, protection from evil,
signifying power over death.
The King of Persia brought him gold
to ensure this one born lowly
would never have to doff his cap,
bow his back, and crack his joints
and hands with a life of working wood.

We anointed his head with oil,
gave bread dipped into wine.
He would be ours for now
(just precious days at Mary's breast or
carried high on my square shoulders.)
Swaddling clothes unfurled,
we shared him with the kneeling beasts.
Ours, for just a heartbeat's breadth at least,
before He became the world's.

Journey to Selfhood

The Body's wisdom

The body has a wisdom and a remembering
in fear, yearning for the safety of the womb.
Any loss of contentment
the stomach registers with unease.
Our kidneys tell when we are peed off,
our back, the load we are carrying,
our liver responds to what sickens us.
Our patient feet record every journey taken;
stony paths, sandy shores and grasses' morning dew.
Our body expresses what we cannot frame in words,
protecting us by growing layers like an oak.
It seeks to expel what it cannot use,
each night cleansing the mind by activating
stray emotions and imagination.
So by listening and cherishing, we grow wise.
Being merely dancers in nature's elements,
we become elements in nature's dance.

Matriarchy

If God knows us from our mother's womb then mothers are goddesses in partnership.

You are more myself than I am comfortable
with.
First joyful namer of my collecting cells
through flesh and cord and thin membrane.
Your voice, the first felt vibration through skin's
walls as you called me my true names.
My names were male and female then,
or both when I was 'little bump'?
I, fickle-finned, fish-quickened limbs protruding,
swam tadpole-like in the first
home ocean and dark amber cave.

My birth was your splitting,
emerging into light,
but you exultant as a lark
saw me only as a pure blast of victory!
Such family joy, that first act upon the human stage.
What luck to fall into love and celebration,
to be passed as a parcel of delight to
grannies, aunties (past childbearing),
and to so many curious-spirited spinsters.

Yours early prayers, cultural history,
first lullabies and nursery rhymes.
Yours the correct calling of body
parts, mine for joy and procreation,
never to be by others owned.
First cheer-leader in the journey of menstruation,
bloodied legs – that you as a child had found
shameful – fertility's proof and
progenitor, time sensitive, moon-blessed.

Closer than life and thought we were.
(We often thought or said the same,
in photographs mistook one for another.)
When did we become defined in opposition?
Sexual competition? Hatred of my teenage self
projecting my wrongness on to your rightness?
Oh! If only you were always 'wrong'.
If only you'd known me less and couldn't see
so clearly what the world had dealt and done to me.

You crafted my weft, weave and web,
cat's cradles, sateen fabric, knitting needles,
eiderdown spreads and hospital-corner-beds,
food feast spreads and HB pencil leads.
Showing how to meld family from lovebirds and
Persian cats, bowls of fish, Spike dogs and
dachshunds.

You my Moira, spinning and mending my injured
soul with sharp pins and delicate needle-point
etching.

Mothers, our first pillow, to drench with warmest
          tears
and beat with angry fists, unjustly to become our
teenage blame cushions, enchanted mirrors
of self-knowledge, and self-disappointment;
broken glass with judgement cutting,
a mother's words reflected into infinity.
We females have to grow beyond this.
There is no right answer, after all,
to 'Who is the Fairest One of All?'

Now, my anchor come loose, my Sybil
(who I pour wax into my ears not to
hear and hear and hear…)
My goddess fallen into fallibility,
my goddess fallen into mortality.

Aged, the skin and veins weaken,
frail body, from which I had grown.
Going into old age, your latest sin
for which I judge harshly, because I so fear
to follow, so fear to lose you.
But surprised by tenderness, for this
newly childlike elder's dependency
I realise that Love is, and always has been, All.

So now graciously and even glamorously
         (as they say)
you persevere. You win over all nurses and carers
with your kindness, (despite my shoddy raked out
love), and show your trademark sureness still,
of good taste, sound sense, wisdom and aplomb.

Lost and Found

I found you happy in the land of lost
and homeless things, the gauntlet glove,
the excess nuts and bolts in your dad's tool shed
(after the engine was fixed.)
Abandoned, your muddied football kit
and studded boots, that 'tall bird's' silver
earring, a trophy on your car's chrome mirror.
Your days lost down the coast with the mods or
happily lost in Spain, your last spree of freedom.
Me the first piece of your how-to-be-an-adult
      jigsaw?
Your completing bracket from an oh-so-
generic self assembly kit?

You found me in the lost land of childhood's things,
still with teddy bears for guardians
my mole-brown velvet riding hat
and the (not-kinky) boots that
needed heaving to remove,
challenged by the gymkhana rosettes,
certificates and pop star's pictures
on my suburban bedroom wall.

Found and Lost

I found myself, after I had
been discarded by someone else

I found you (because for F's sake somebody
had to)

I found Jesus when I
didn't know he was lost

I found a friend in you because
no-one else would have me

I found these words – once words
were futile

I lost my way when accommodating yours

Find here, a lost and found life
of shore-line beach-combing.

Away to School

Boarding at Mystic House School

Boarding for The Daughters of Gentlewomen

Looming, cliff-perched
ready to interrogate this
skimpy, shaking new child with
'sort your hair out'
untameability.
Portentous trunks for ghoul-grey
hooded capes and large gusseted
woolly blue gym knickers.
Arrival survival? The school head,
owl-like, loved a good crime drama,
was ever jolly, no arsenic in her old lace
nor embroidering emotions.
No patron saints of domesticity
in her study, pictures of the first
national women's cricket team,
war-time Lake District 'gals' these future
stalwart women, in bifurcated garments
smiling leathered and willowed.

Through the open window, barbarian cries,
far playing fields waging lacrosse and hockey wars,

tribal calls as pigtails swung and wooden weapons
flashed and swished while music carried
from creaky uprights and dusty grands.

We renegades and co-conspirators would
conceal less upright music in dorm,
pirate radios and record-deck-sneaking.
Our flower-power hammer or nail protest songs.
Getting stoned on life and mayhem for
all those spinsters so past their prime and
none of them a Jean Brodie.

Prisoners, we awaited 'outs' weekends
held secret séances, avoided the haunted,
and the uglifying mirrors. Cloaked and hooded
apparitions dogged us, alongside fervent visions of
Arthurian holiness. Vigils held for vocation
and dreams of mystic Avalon.
Praying all night for worthiness to lead and spells
to ward off the witches on the downs.

Dry shampoo and greasy hair,
Bathing once a week in cold cast-iron,
niggardly greened brass dispensing
inches of chalky luke-warm water.
Babes in the dorm, drinking sham – Babycham,
stories whispered, musicals rehearsed,
a bra draped over the ceiling lamp, us
singing in chorus!

Midnight feasts (pheasant nabbed from
Daddy's shoot), dehydrated rice dishes
(partly reconstituted in pencil cases),
all eaten nearly warm and just before
the invention of sex and salmonella.
Up all night, playing truant, jacks and guitars.

So now the mystic fates have departed,
the shuttle dropped, the skein has ended
but the tapestry remains.
Thus our fated and fêted girlhoods were
unfurled and spun and ended here.
In all those exultant, myriad, woven marvels
Our Jerusalem was founded here!

It already has

I am that child doing a twirl in her
many petticoated velvet party-dress,
of broderie anglaise, clouds, flowers and butterflies,
confident as a colt, frisky as a kid
the eager-to-please one who wants
to do it right to blaze a trail,
to make that entrance.

I'd love to leave it there but
then life goes differently,
with its prat falls and trip wires
its banana skies and mud pies
with my open wide eyes, my hooded
Mona Lisa style eyes and nervous smile.

'I'd like to wipe that look off your face girl'
'stop smirking - stop blathering - stop snivelling'
'what are you up to? I'll give you "thinking" '
'I'll tell you what "reading" does for you..'
'Talk back and I'll wash your mouth out with soap'
'I'll pull your pants down and give you what for'.

Later a shuttered teen, closed like a trap
a tad round-shouldered, no longer skipping,
idly kicks the soggy fallen leaves, and hears a
chirpy, blokey workman call from on high,
'Cheer up love, it may never happen.'

Heroes and Camp Followers

Hero Worship

I am old enough to know
and yet I keep on slipping
on the muddy puddles
around your feet
of clay.

You cannot be different from what you are
any more than I.
We should know by now
the games
people play.

I put you on that pedestal
knowing every time
it'll be something
you do, get, want
or say.

Why do I expect
better or the best
possible versions
of those
I love
anyway?

All the amazing ones that I will not be

No-one can have 360 degree vision
is why we need each other's
 sight.
We all carry around our
own miniature universes
 But
like cruciformed God or burdened Hercules
alone it is too heavy.

From a Family Album

Female Suffrage

Maternal Great-Grandmother.
Strong, imperious, courageous.
Virginia Wolfe eyes, cloaked and colour changing,
drawing you in to a world of sentiment and art,
needle point séances and tales of tea with Royalty.
Always moving on, ever homemaking, fleeing
poverty, murderers and other dire circumstances.
Secret suffragette, coded banners and jewellery,
Claimed seventh child of the seventh child,
expert at entertaining, operetta, spinning curses,
both telling (and losing) fortunes.
A beautiful body once, I imagine,
lithe, curved, no straight lines, a perfect artist's
        model.
With breasts to cleave to, loved
for their hug and their swing and sway.
With her own rhythm and feet made to dance
in tightest shoes, and direst circumstances
(her descendants could dance their tarantella
in killer stilettos.) The next generation found her
an impressively melancholic witch weaving
cautionary spells and dressed in traffic-stopping garb
of blackest obsidian, spinel and spangled jet.

Great Grandmother Louise, Poverty

Per aspera ad astra: through hardships to the stars

Not strong enough for this world, they said.
Delicate and fey, angelic, fairy child,
mother of my infant grandfather.
Near transparent with tuberculosis, thoughts
wandering, her large water-colour eyes
were purest sky, her demeanour gentle.
Violets, catkins and soft pussy willow clouds
      were her loved colours.
Ethereal enchantress played the mandolin
for her own changeling spell.
Child's hands and feet, little face and dainty waist.
Victorian Heroine, sacrificial working class woman,
fell, into widowhood and poverty,
but never out of respectability.
Louise, in my photo of you, I see you had so few
      choices,
so loved, so sad a life, gave to me life.
Hagiographically we treasure you still.

Beating rugs and Hitler

She, the up-to-mischief sister,
borrowed a party dress to
walk out with my granddad Fred
at chestnut blossom time.
They were married a respectable year
later, another year before
the young Fred came along.

Dust or gloom stood no chance in her path
with her old apron on (the same one,
pale, floral, thin with washing) and
hair tied back, with a Kirby grip or two.
Armed with a rag, a washboard and a
bucketful of suds, she could
take on the world.
No wonder Hitler was defeated.
He had no plans for the indomitable
Mum's Army.

Her beliefs in life were, family,
food (resolutely cooked to submission)
and cleanliness.
Her recruits bicarb', washing soda,

Bronco toilet paper
(the soft indicated weakness of constitution)
and (of course!) coal tar soap.
Everyone rigorously lathered hair to toe
behind ears and in all crannies,
til disinfected and squeaking
skin became so very pink
while soft and sweet as milk.
Her regime was hygiene not female vanity
uniformly dictating
the wearing of vests, thickly
gusseted knickers, girdles,
and ribbed cotton brassieres.
(Tights viewed as sinful germ harbours,
flaunted by floozies.)
All stockings were Darjeeling coloured, defending
decency with elastic bands for garters.

Beds were bridal in purity where tautly folded
white cotton sheets nudged plump feather
        eiderdowns.
After seeing off Hitler, Spike the jaunty dog
(and poor Fred's advances)
she worked off her elder years in family shops
and market stalls, coaxing a gleam
from buxom melons, mangos and apples.
Grandma of my memory, of the forget-me-not eyes
whose bosom was my best refuge,
is always cleaning with suds and gusto,

always cooking vegetables and baking.
Crumbling pastry layers enfolding apple, sloppy
banana custards, golden cake encased in
transparent butter paper heavy with fruit.
But sometimes, best of all, at weddings,
just letting herself go!
Once more the dress-thief at the Poly dance,
dancing the Okey-Cokey, dangling a toddler or two
in a mad "Diddly, Diddly Do" jig!
always getting tipsy on 'just one
port and lemon please'. And at these dos I see Kate,
the stalwart, the puritan, the proud
home guard-man's wife, so rarely caught out,
now doubled over and dissolved
in laughter.

My Aunty, The Peace Warrior

pax optima rerum: peace is the greatest good

Standing foursquare under an archer's star,
kind eyes, your arrows, aimed at the future.
Visionaries' banners
were home sewn and stitched
by sore soul fingers with heart's own fibres.
They read "The Family of Man" "Make Love Not
War" and banning the bomb you became
a warrior horse maiden with hidden armour.
Arm in arm campaigning in duffle coats,
headscarves and slacks, with Mowlem and Kent our
aunty marched, singing not slacking.
You lived intensely, alternatively, among the
      ordinary,
banging tin pots and pans against annihilation of
this green and pleasant land.

Ireland, and Greenham, songs summoned you with
      forever fellowship
of those who cared enough to stand together so
      others could live.
Thereafter charging windmills far larger than your
      whole world.

Rocinante carried you farther than your own
    expansive vision
to hold the hand of the first space woman, to share
food with the Soviet Mothers for Peace.
Leaving your own suburban home
To see dreams of hope in a Russian child's eyes
you pushed against humanity's darkness
and wished for more love than this world could
    hold.
When women circumnavigated politics to birth
    change
You were a midwife.

From different times, I salute you, brave centaur, you can now run free.

They have your heart

They are designed
to win and then
to break your heart
not over all that
poo-ing and chewing
that rug-come-work-of-art.

Unlike foxes they do not live
for a few seasons.
They enter your family
with no warning that
you will love them beyond reason.
They become family, best friends
and share every outing.
Outings are ordered by them.

Programmed to protect
Such soft little things
we start off that way and then realise
how they are programmed to protect us.
Not only hearth and home but you, your family
they would die for.

Cruelly, they live a short life
but that life is all your Sundays,
spare time, connecting us with nature.

They may be only politer wolves
but they do not dissemble.
Their loyalty is beyond treasure.

If there is a heaven they will be there first.
Imagine! The wagging of tails, purrs, licks
and cacophony of welcoming barks!

Religiosity and Faith

Fool's choices

(I couldn't sell my soul, so I just gave it away in small pieces...)

The fool didn't find his soul a good fit.
(A garment as vast as the universe
just wasn't fashionable).
You couldn't accessorize culpability and contrition.
The capacity for infinite compassion
(makes more than your bum look big.)
Of course they never read the maker's manual
to find the applications – kept it on the shelf.

*(Perhaps this 'soul' may have some value one day
on somewhere like eBay?)*

Salt, Psalter and sacrilege

They taught me sin and seven deadly pleasures
but inside my heart still grew a cave of praise.
Golden bowls of eyes overfilled,
glory like angel illuminations feathering my prayers.
Ululations, Halley Halley Hallelujahs – bursting
through the firmament, the congregation hands and
      eyes raised
singing in tongues the purest praise.
Praise for the day, praise for the harvest
of warm winter socks, of conkers and sweet
      chestnuts
in cases prickly as pain and silky as delight.

Songs heaven winged, sound soaring,
marvel upon marvel your burden becomes light
when shared with the Numberer of Stars,
the carer for the tiniest fallen bird,
the feeder of hungry, gatherer of the lost.

But praise preachers were not simple men those
      days.
I yearned to meet that Shepherd among lilies,
of crusty loaves, fallen birds and slippery fishes.

St Francis and St Ambrose my hippy calling,
communing with nature, shy hares and soft-eyed
    seals.

Guilt-and-fear-men they were, set to hobble bodies
and blind eyes, with wenches' belts, nags' bridles,
and the game of walking on hot stones, and the
    floating
of wise women by those without wisdom.
Women should not talk in church, they said.
Woe-men, godsips, and gossips, heads covered
should be covered by a man. Circumcisions
could be performed on the child's body
or on the naked soul.

Hallelujah hypocrites

The Elder with the fabulous feeling-you-up eyes.
The Elder, who casts the stone and makes sure it
has 'hellstone' and 'brimstone' and 'headstone' and
'bedstone' inscribed on its surface.
The Elder preaching the delights of chastity
and the marriage bed of sanctity and the joy of
    purity.
Who relishes those acts which do not constitute
    adultery.
The Elder who scorns thought as a sin,
as Eve's apple and snare (and Adam's curse)
his serpent of sensual delight to be ground
    underfoot.

The smiting Elder who sees love as punishment
    written into the universe.
The laughing Elder who is the wolf beneath the
    sheep,
beneath the jolly bon viveur.
Those seeming kind who take in the imperfect to
demonstrate the perfection of their wealth and
    fortune.
The praying and baptising Elder who mantis-like
seeks out his prey with care, a lone woman, boy or
child out of their depth who he then symbolically
    holds under.
The Elder who is relatable to and weak, forever
confessing his sins, while revelling in self-pity.
The Elder of indulgences, indulging in
self-satisfaction and smugness.
The Elder of conversion therapy of exorcisms
and excoriation of the injured soul.

He whose feet walked humbly among the
prostituted, walked barefoot by the water,
walked in poverty, hung out with lepers, was
    none of the above.
From these spouting men and their obediently
knitted myopically kind wives, may All That's Holy
    save us.

Riddle

*What can't be bought or loaned
but can always be lost or found?*

Faith, a conundrum?
   While fragile and precarious,
a thing of cobwebs, cricket wing homilies,
and bird breast-bone wishes.

Made of thoughts, of breath, of light,
actually, of nothing strong enough
to build bridges with.
Yet its purpose is as a breaker of despair
and maker of the new imaginings, way-finder
and burden carrier.
Our co-creation, human's Godly work?

Faith, a friend and mother of
this walk of stones,
sibling of Hope and Love both,
child of anguished doubt and steadfast belief.
Beyond experience, before proof,
it's the first step to walk on the water
to foot-find the invisible bridge in the air.
It enables us to unfurl wings, to fly, to begin to pedal
free, leaving the steadying parent's grip.

Opposite of desire, it is always beyond the
monkey who cannot release her clutched nut.
And we are all that seduction-sickened
and faithless monkey.

Faith needs to be summoned or gifted
to be within our power, it comes
invisibly when nothing else is there.
Apparent in a good parent's
or teacher's love, and in
all who had faith in you, formed You.

Fostered in fellowship it is an inspiration
a fingertip grasping on life's edge.
It can only ever be just enough,
there is not more than is needed.
Belief in light at the end of the tunnel,
sun following rain, knowing before seeing.
Like elven food or fairy gold it disappears
at the end of the day to be sought anew.

We call the glass-half-full 'optimism' but when
the glass is empty Faith relates the re-filling.
When hope has fled it is just a tiny spark and
even beyond that, it finds light beyond the
last candle's holy life.
Commonly our daily bread, and
uncommon nurture when all else fails us.
Faith visits in the guise of a leper

or a king, a lion or a mouse,
in a cloud's wisp or a mountain,
a single star point, light years away,
a precious jewel or sodden ground.
She is the anchorite who tells us of
all of the manner of things which shall be well,
an earth-moving giant, while still the
humble supplicant with her begging bowl.
The opposite of dogma, or observance,
a wild, triumphant flowering of stale Theism.
Faith, an infant outcast crosses human boundaries
and miraculously recognises and doubles itself
with Joy in other foot-sore wanderers.

The Impossibility of Faith

It does exist in the old stories,
of the good, for the good, by the good,
stronger than steel, they say.
The stuff of heroism and crucifixions,
indicating that the good in us
is the God in us, and being something
elusively winged, resembles Love.
Faith, they say, is from outside of time,
so even while naked, tied and blinded, she
can see more clearly than Hope.
Plato's den is our world of light and spectacle
and Faith says, merely reflects a truer, realer deal.
This healer of souls and impossible warrior is
translator of our faded myths and
dusty hieroglyphics to Life beyond, unknown.

Mental Health and Fundamentalism in the 1970s

Unarguably a cartoon school girl,
gym slip tied with a karate belt,
tie awry, battered school hat,
crazy bunches of bushy hair,
constantly displaying your brightness,
your daring and your cotton underwear.
Undoubtedly our super hero,
they suggest you were
already fleeing mania's steel claws?
Impersonations had us in stiches but
later had you in a straitjacket?
Surreality of visions, addictions, voices
mockingly just out of reach.
Sometime neglected, abused, derided,
you were never able to trust love.
I shrunk from that other landscape and
your mental population, that I couldn't see.
I wasn't there to hold your veil, your head or hand,
both launching into adulthood too early.

Married, marked and marred in red,
beaten, pregnant and maddened all in that same
> year.
First fed to vengeful demons of religious
fundamentalism then finally, fatally, lost to echoing
institutions.

The sheer weight of things

Sometimes my knees buckle
under the sheer weight of stuff.

For the sheer weight of traffic
there are calming measures;
allowances are made,
sympathy is proffered.
Not so for the sheer weight of things.

A woodworker
having served an apprenticeship
way into middle age calls out.
'Come here all you overloaded –
aren't those invisible burdens a bugbear?
Thoughts of stuff you cannot
change, stuff done wrong,
stuff you can never mend,
sheer weight of stuff to do,
the sheer weight of stuff is too heavy.'
'My burden is light,' said he,
'See, yours too can be lightened
for a backpack of the soul
no space is needed.'

Fanciful Time Travel

Hey Diddle Diddle

Scientists, folk tales and gothic yarns
spin stories of super-moons, red
or blue as the artist's back-drop for
the howling-wolf's-ache.
Creamy like pitted porridge, the bovine leaper's
joy, and the midnight romancer's passion.
Luna/Aega the goddess moon
dances in harmony with
spuming tides and golden harvest.
A baby, fish-like, quickens and is birthed
by the moon's procreative rhythms.
Diana/Artemis dramatically hides
and reveals herself to telescopes.
In India silver Candi rides the night
(while golden Chandra charioteers the sun.)
This cheesy moon delights in astrolabes and
In festive spilling of coloured dyes and spices.
Perseid meteorites strike our moon,
like cosmic hail, and star nurseries,
milkily-birth mini-moons.
Our striptease goddess, conversant
with the many moons of Mars, Saturn,
Jupiter and Uranus claims –
'For this earth I can do better still,
a spectacular moon that can blow your mind
just every now and again, just once in a while…'

Baby, I may be biased?

I see you as an extraordinary happening.
    An incredibly unique cosmic occurrence,
    radiant and fine
    as Volcanic lightning, Snow donuts and Fire
    Rainbows.

Lenticular clouds, Auroras and Firewhirls
compete with your new beauty.
Frost flowers, Light poles and Morning glory clouds,
Water spouts and Mammatus clouds
are not more marvellous.

Hessdalen lights and Brinicles,
Earthquake brights and Sailing stones,
raining animals, fish or frogs
do not hold a cosmic candle
to your extraordinary bioluminescence.
Baby, I may be biased but
you are certainly and always will be
the best to me of all that's audacious and heroical.

The Eighth

Waking or dreaming? I'm somewhere between
worlds. Now drowning in my own stink
Slipping into memories or nightmares
Ghosts, ghouls and goodwives taunt me
So many called Thomas, where are their heads?
I feel their hands on me and dread a throttling
But they cool my pillow, refresh my nosegays,
or put me on the rack of physic and bandage
      changing.
I ask them to leave some skin but skin has gone to
      pulp.
The most admired hams, the best-turned ankle
Feet light as panther's (so my brides would say)
made for a jig, primed for a galliard.
Soon will they come too for my head?

Strangely now I pine for the old tongue
Can it signify that a king should hear the same
prayers as a cleaner of latrines?

Ha, as God's divine prince – we share a joke or two
On women and Priests! My undoing.

Now, I am shriven, it seems I miss them all,
the dancing eyes of comely Anne
Her last laugh – a gash caused by the axe?

They live with me each day, one tends my hair
another begs a reel, one's perfume fills my head,
the other a pair of long green sleeves.
We kept a lively court, it was the best in
      Christendom,
and I the comely prince most ready for the game.

Visions come as dying men may see
(For sighted eyes do dim, the brain
makes demons of our senses.)
Will there be another Hal blessed with my
strawberry hair? So loved, so courted?
Would he exert his will against advice of fools?
Good luck to him – Ha, it is a godly jest, this way
to end, weak as a baby in his crib,
Our royal person dabbed, daubed and dibbled.
Ahem! How I have lived! How well will be
      remembered.

Noah before the rainbow

While Noah prayed and scanned the horizon
Mrs Noah fed the animal kingdom.
The sixty species of rats had fallen out
with sixty of the species of bats
and the meat-eaters were looking hungrily
at the grass-eaters, who whimpered,
whinnied or wittered.

The dinosaur was harrumphing.
The dire wolf, the dodo and the Tasmanian tiger
would not settle.
Shem, Ham and Japeth were also
unruly, complaining that this diet
of herbs and grain was not sufficient
for the duty of
repopulating the earth.

The lone unicorn sighed
"You think you have troubles?"
The Shar Pei had grown extra
frown-lines.

I'm not telling tales here
But Ham was not vegetarian
(especially once the vegetables
aged and grew beards.)
He's the one I'd point my finger at,
when Emzara, wife of Noah, came
to groom the unicorn and found –
only a single horn.

Three Troublesome Old Men

The Cedars Retirement Home
found them hard to manage.
Xi, Don and Vlad had remarkable
personality disorders.
Don trying to grab nurses' pussies.
Vlad persisting in taking off his shirt
and throwing shit around.
Xi locked the cleaners in the cupboard.

They had no comprehension
of how to share.
In occupational therapy
Don building with Lego
would not let Vlad enlarge
his construction,
Xi was the only one who played
quietly on his own.

Temper tantrums
were dealt with firmly.
Matron laid down the
rules that there would be no biscuits
for those calling out offensive names,

snatching, or stealing;
there would be absolutely no violence
or blaming someone else.
Within a month they had
learned how to play nicely.
Don was getting good at knitting
Vlad was into cooking
and Xi had taught them all origami.
Amazing what a bit of old-fashioned
discipline and common sense can achieve.

Old Mother Time

More sinister than Father Time she seems,
pointing that crooked finger, leering with
her bleary eye.
Old Mother Time has her knitting needles,
winding sheet, net or poison,
with perhaps, her spoonful of sugar?

Sister of St Catherine, of the wheel of fate
or of the three Furies with their delicate thread?
Is she the same hag who sat by the guillotine,
Madame Defarge, the tricoteuse? Did she knit our
names into her blanket, and revolutionaries' hats of
blood? Does she dance the dance of death
(in those red shoes), hand-holding her partner
in her merry death grip?

Is she the red-haired, red-robed angel
of retribution, a screaming-blue-murder banshee?

Is she the She spider, Ariadne eating her partner?
Or the Sibyl who wanted immortality
but forgot about the curse of aging?
Both beautiful and monstrous like Shiva,
unlike Father Time she has no scythe.

New Year arrives, infant Mother Time holds
her timepiece, an hourglass and
mortals' precious companion, she becomes
good-mother of human experience and life.

Unbound by our contraptions,
forever reborn anew, we have her kinship
only for our brief span. We cannot cheat
her but she, feeling niggardly, can short-change us.

Mother Time, you are to living souls
as fickle as nature, as shifting as thought, as
mysteriously cursed and blessed as consciousness.

One Tree Hill

Today we walked on One Tree Hill.
The tree now just a woody crown
of weathered teeth from blackened ground
a spot for bonfires drugs and vapes,
a place for teens without a home?

In memory once a mighty oak
for multitudes that creep or fly
the squirrel's dray, the pigeons poke,
the jay and magpie's treasure hoard,
rough warren for all rabbits shy.

In time it's seen royal hunts and harts
with antlers fit to deck royal halls.
It's seen the war-time squadrons fly
and farm boys marching off to wars.

First hollowed out by age and time
then burnt by vandals to be sure
this Kingly Oak should be defaced
so fools can prattle, laugh and boast
that majesty would rule no more?

Today we saw the circle still
the space where lived a heart of oak
we saw the debris of bored youth,

porn mags, a glove without its mate,
discarded bottles, cans and smokes.

What calls these revellers to this spot?
What comfort gives the blackened ground?
When dozing by a dancing flame
what ghosts rise up in fields around?
Does One Tree Oak protect and guard,
lone sentinel through times unknown,
Invisibly present, still hearth and home?

Un-pathetic fallacy poem 2020

Un-churched, un-mosqued,
Un-templed and un-shuled.
Un-dated, un-work-placed and un-schooled
Un-christened, un-community-ed and un-married
Un-shrived, un-communioned, then
Un-ceremoniously un-buried.

Denied our holy places, our communities,
our families, our hot dates, our play dates,
some became pantheists, birds as messengers
in tranquil empty skies, unbearable beauty in
a fallen leaf on a silent muddy footpath,
a new shoot in a scrap of broken soil.

We changed to live online, on screen,
TV the cosy/slippery rabbit warren
we all fell into. Surrogate emotions,
thrills for experience.
Spring/Summer/Winter/Autumn Murders
(to prevent us murdering each other?)
Orwell's 'proletarian feed' after all.
The six sins of vanity, greed, sloth,
envy, gluttony and lust, thrived

on such marketing, the seventh, wrath
raged from defeated expectation when instant
gratification gave diminishing hits.
Shopping, eating and fucking were indoor
addictions, walking and nature-watching
the only prescribed 'get out of jail' predilections.

How many true-love possibilities were lost
as sex was banned with those outside
your household? (So incest was OK then?)
The bold and the lonely (we were all lonely)
went people-shopping for their dates.
Clicking and swiping for hook-ups?
Your online selfie – just another fuck-up?

Many saw highest humanity, saw rainbows
and a way beyond prejudice.
This was the time (it seemed) to
examine all lives to value, question,
and to choose humanity.
To write poetry or family histories?
Something righteous betwixt Life and Mammon?
We sought answers to all the vexed questions,
all rights and wrongs, as our leaders let us down.
For what are human beings without each other,
are we any more than our own best interests,
our noble or nefarious deeds,
our doings and un-doings,
our comings and our goings?

Off To War

From the Belgium French War Graves

Bedford Cemetery

Warr Meets Peace

In tribute to Michael Morpurgo, author of 'Private Peaceful'
August 2004

By a cow pool
in fields of ripening corn
where electric-blue dragonflies
and prehistoric herons
dip, hover or in vigil stand
Peaceful, Sergeant,
in cold stone masonry
is circled round
by children
studying war
so there will be war no more?

A Sergeant Warr
and Sergeant Battle
also lay nearby
and Sergeant Peace.
Military names no tourist parties seek.

Once, perhaps smiling, did they share
a billet and a roll of baccy,
or covering a drowning face from
gas's searing reek yanked one to safety from
the pull of trench water and fouled mud?
Or did they pass each other without a nod
like bloodied, walking, vacant ghosts
along the tunnelled way as in this earth,
Battle, Warr, and Peace
civilly meet in death?

Tyne Cot

Roses' scent, poppy-red and sweet,
fragrances the air where
these young warriors sleep.

What could awake them?
When Arthur comes again?
At England's hour of need?
The army of the slain?

Will the Last Post
bring home once more
to cot and byre these soldiers
from Europe's golden hills or pebbled shores?

Or to Stanley Spencer's garden paradise
this Tyne Cot might become a portal wide?
And thus those fallen souls may rise
to stand on guard at a Greater Gardener's side?

These comforting tales we murmur still
despite new wasted crush of youth,
I will believe them, if you will.
Too awful is actual blooded truth.

Forgive

Forgive us (poor neglected shades,
twice broken, unwound, slain),
we who tread among
your treasured spilled remains.

We the (almost) tourists
pause and maybe shiver
with moth-touch of a farm boy's
forgotten name,
bidden from the wind,
as at the snuffing of a flame,
recapturing his groan and call.

Trophies, unearthed by recent farmer's sweat,
His precious bones, his buckle from a belt?

We feel the same caressing breeze
raising red petals' tiny spilled seeds.
The names, John, George and Tim, are
laid in sunshine in honour of their deeds.
The names, Wolfgang, Peter, Karl,
as invaders, crammed in dusty border,
we shake our heads at the sheer number,
here who in anguish fought then fell.

The March

This is a personal response after being honoured to talk to 'Bunny' Loughlin, my uncle Hugh's dad, who was one of 300,000 POW Veterans. He was a survivor of the 100,000 or so who after up to five years of imprisonment and hard labour on railways & in coal mines on Eastern front Czechoslovakia or Poland marched up to 1,000 miles for three months or more in temperatures of minus thirty with little food to scavenge.

No telling those who found us on the road
remains of men, mere fallen boughs
bound round with rancid rags.
So many of us frozen in the night,
victims of that ancient sign of light,
horrors upon horrors, hidden,
(while in watchful sight).

Travelling, those worse off than us
a crazy land where stripped
(as if for sleep)
Christ's people herded
to a crime so deep.

We never forget those passersby;
the lost, abandoned, all too tired to cry
once musicians, mothers, babes,

sensitive faces and expressive hands
eyes unblinking, lost in Hell's cold lands.

January '45, began this march of death
mocking our victories over bleak despair
we left the sadism of man back there
for uncaring nature's worsening care.
No more guards, no being pushed around,
instead shared trudging over hardest ground.

Foot dragged in front of foot
fatal to trip o'er branch or root.
Heads down, breath turning into ice flowers
on lapels and lashes, bitter passing hours.
Every move costing courage dear
breeding something still disguised as cheer
(stubborn will and cussed British fortitude.)

We helped each other, each an 'oppo'.
Keeping up morale from dogged habit
annoying and confounding our captors too
like Vera flipping Lynn still singing through
while tending our bleeding, our bandaged,
our blackened hands, feet and faces,
putting us through our feckin' paces.

Food? We took the bone from the dog,
the swill from the pigs, the rotten turnip from the
hog.

Casting an eye at a pretty girl, 'Like to dance a jig?'
(she danced the Hitler Youth rifle punch instead
for her smile) we carried that sight,
mile on mile on mile.
In the end we did not give in, that's all
it was really, and how we got through at all
the thick, and mostly, bloody thin.

From being frozen as brass monkeys' nuts,
luck, prayer, Red Cross parcels, sound boots,
took us to banners, bands and flippin' doughnuts.
From a country worth trudging a thousand miles for
we found what crawling man can somehow do.
Was freedom worth their suffering paid and more,
with or without bright medals to thank you?

Walks and Wanderings

Winter Spell

Ice glazed in a puddle-window,
a bright fern's fronds uncurled crook
plays chimerical gold disguise.

Walking on, marking the snow,
an acer leaf, redder than wine,
my unread document.
A parchment leaf twists
over and over on the
soft iced pillows, drawing a
line to a small bird's
fine etched footprints.

The silence is profound,
the whisper of slight flurries
blurs all edges. The air is sharp
with a blue that can be inhaled
and warmth hangs in the air like
part-erased wings of angels.

Autumn's dance

The swirl of sycamore
the hand span of sweet bright maple,
the plash of chestnut's umbels,
grenades of fallen pods, flail-headed.

Fig trees drop their modest clothing
a striptease to display
well hung figs and figlets
their swollen insides tender-red,
softly, sweetly, intimate.

The falling, full-bodied sheen
of apples red and gold
shining bounty for fox, magpie,
hodgepodge and slug.
Firm, marvellous sweet,
giving into boozy cider's
dizzying gift of potent rot.
Our pigeon waddles tipsy,
a dapper gentleman home to his nest.

From vine on garden wall
to sunlight through park railings
an ecstatic marvel.
The Plane tree goddess
discarding leaves and maces

swaying her plathed and
patched beauty in flirtatious winds.
Mist silver, greyed or yellowed,
this autumn smudges and paints
these late impressionistic days
of fabulous, flurrying, fleeting, farewells.

A disturbance

Where do birds sleep?
On the spindly,
dwindling tops of trees.
Seven here for a secret,
until a cat's creep
unpacked the branches
of ragged black and white
with a flap and flutter.

Two clattered away
leaving five 'for silver'
as ruffled guards.
The cat, as ever,
dropped down
now not as clever
and licked her paws
seeking easier prey.

The remaining murder
of magpies
chatter and clatter.
Our portly pigeon
posted like a spy
watches them scatter,
head under taupe wing
listens to their cry,

a suburban subaltern,
he trembles slightly on his single
wisp-top sprout.

Too much Awesomeness in Banff

'That would be awesome ma'am' he said (when I asked if I could pay in cash).
'What are those mountains there?' I asked
'The seven sisters,' he proudly grinned.
'They are awesome' I said.

Journeys to Creativity

The Cynic's Guide to Art?

What is poetry? Transubstantiation?
Does it require explanation or validation?
Or is it after all only mental masturbation?
What is Art? An act of alchemy?
Or – just wanking about with imagery really?

Poems – catch 'em before they fly

Jump high! Use your best and longest net,
catch them while you don't forget!
These butterflies will soon depart, before your pen
can even start, leaving merely
a vacant plot in the (unreliable)
poetry region of your heart.

The Poet

The poet sees the moon
through the cherry tree
(on the night before
the start of spring).

He sees a ball or a balloon
caught in the dark branches.
He sees a maiden peering through
the blushing blossom.
He sees a merry farmer, or a hunter,
a silver dish or golden orb
competing with the sun.

The moon reflects the light
steadily, unmoved, replete.
From the cerulean sky
through pink blossom corollas
it shines on poet and prophet,
on astrologer and astronomer,
scientist, selenologist,
and all us poor metaphor-makers,
earthlings and dreamers.

The Muse

My muse passes the opposite way
I see her in a train window beckoning.
Her face slides down the wall.
Her hands are cut from brambles
her nails broken.
She is neglected and I admit
I have starved her…
She is a touch golden or perhaps green
a shape changer who (if minded)
can become my own jewelled
tortoise or unbroken stallion.

Journeys Home

When I should go

When I should go, search for me
in the green shades where
the king cups grow
in orange flow, wild garlic
and white anemone nod and quiver.
Later bonnets of mauve balsam blows
along the sky-reflecting pebbled river.

Where fairy houses can be glimpsed
among the stately beeches' folds
and knolls and creases,
and bluebells make caps for tiny heads,
fly agarics their tables,
dragonflies resplendent steeds,
fern fiddle heads their stables.

Find me in the books I loved,
the imagery, the poetry,
and in every favourite record's hit,
the flow, the heart's chemistry,
my water dragon self, playing Tai Chi,
and not because I loved them all but
because I lived with true intensity.

If I should lose you, if I should lose myself,
the memory gone down unknown paths,

remember and experience deeply, all I
have forgot, is all that I can rightly ask.

Remember for me the river's sky,
the earth's peaty hold,
the fields of sunlight, beckoning gold,
your warmth my body loved to hug and hold.

Blessings

Bless your every wish to bless
May your blessings always
Fall on grateful soil
May your blessings come home
To bless you and may they multiply
Bless your water journey
Otter swift from paw to shore
Bless your aura may it bring light and delight
Bless the atmosphere you inhabit
May you move through it with strength and grace
Bless the fire in your hearth and heart
May your warmth draw goodness towards you
Bless the darkness may it be your place of solace
Bless the earth you till and the seeds you sow
May flowers and fruit follow your footfall
Bless your hands to comfort, shape and heal
Bless those you bless passing through your life
Bless those who come in gladness to your door
Bless those who bless you
Bless those who can't, whose cup is empty
May you know who can be rescued
Who to hold or to let go
Bless and lighten your every inspiration to bless
You are a child of blessings.

Notes from the author

It is with some irony that this book on journeys begins with poems about home, everyone's first formative nest and springboard. Many of my poems are based on childhood experiences of the cosy, firmly female realm of 1950s to later partnering up and entering a more male environment.

These poems are more autobiographical than in my first book 'Poems For Life's Stages' but representations of real people are always fictionalised to convey a wider message.

Indulging in time travel, I have mused on journeys made by historical 'ghosts' along with the larger than life aspects of some of my own family.

Many of life's major transitions are not represented, one of the greatest being that of parenthood. Perhaps this is because these other poems are still somewhere in the ether, waiting to find me.

In the same way that the Romantic poets have little in common with my life but are still so edifying, my stories are not similar to younger readers' lives but I hope the emotions can still resonate and enrich.

In my mind we are all pilgrims picking up specks and crumbs of things we need along the way so when I decided to compile these poems, all written and returned to over a period of years, the word 'journeys' as a way of viewing our experiences seemed a good fit rather than a cliché. I hope it does still.

Isn't life, with its bizarre pit stops, crashes and detours, more extraordinary and serendipitous than one could ever imagine? Gratitude teaches me to never take things for granted, because nothing, however wrong or right, is forever. I believe that my own guiding angels must have a great sense of absurd humour alongside their main job of eternally resonating love.

If you have, thank you for reading my poems and hopefully mulling over them, and I love to imagine that my readers might also be inspired to write. Please do keep reading and buying poetry, we need to keep this art alive and relevant. I do urge you to read across the ages, because there is such joy in grasping a poem by Blake or Betjeman and then switching forward in time to relish poems by marvellous contemporaries such as Daljit Nagra, Jackie Kay or Liz Berry.

Wishing you the very best of journeys and wherever life takes you both way bread and way blessings.

Thank yous

Thank you brilliant Howard Phillips, for being a midwife to this volume. All complied, combed through and checked for typos and textual errors, you were still able to find some slips and more work for me to do, looking critically with expert sensitivity to verse and language. Your questioning helped me finesse this work and to sometimes simplify and sometimes elaborate, to get to my truth. You are a talented enabling teacher and your pupils over the years surely didn't realise their fortune having always your best and gently luminous attention.

Thank you brave Juliet Morris, for being my first reader just as these poems, having jostled for their place, had become a volume and for doing the most tedious first proofing job.

Thank you wonderful Susan Luckett for taking on the mantel. Without such eagle eyes my dyslexic typos and grammatical mistake-blindness would've been more screamingly evident.

Thank you dear Melanie Low again for remaining my true critical, poetical, inspirational proofreading friend.

Thank you too to the gifted author and artist, Ian C.P. Irvine for being (even posthumously) your witty and creative self and proving to be the bravest human being I've known. Also for your insistence that I should get my work published and for generously giving away your own writing secrets in your motivational book 'Get Writing'.

Lastly a heartfelt **thank you** to Katharine Smith and Heddon Publishing without whom this would never have become more than just words on the cloud and in the wind. Thank you for your trusty editorship and zen-like patience. **Thank you** also to Catherine Clarke for beautiful artwork expressing my love of life's twisty, turny, and rarely on-course journeys.

www.ingramcontent.com/pod-product-compliance
Lightning Source LLC
Chambersburg PA
CBHW060457080526
44584CB00015B/1454